The Story of the Ingalls Family

by William Anderson

Little House on the Prairie
Independence, Kansas

Foreword

Since the original version of *The Story of the Ingalls Family* was published more than twenty years ago, an additional mass of facts, historic writings, oral history and documentation has enriched my bulging archives on the family Laura Ingalls Wilder made so real in the pages of her "Little House" books.

When doing the initial research on the roots and relatives of Laura Ingalls Wilder as an elementary student, I had no idea what "oral history" was. But fortunately, as Thoreau would say, I acted "in the nick of time" by interviewing dozens of Ingalls friends, neighbors and relatives, both in person and in correspondence. Most of those generous, gracious people are gone now, but their impressions and anecdotes remain. Some of them I'll share here for the first time.

Seven summers working with the Laura Ingalls Wilder Memorial Society's activities in De Smet, South Dakota greatly enhanced my knowledge of the town's most famous family. Further sleuthing in the Black Hills filled in the gaps of the Ingalls story as it happened in western South Dakota. Rose Wilder Lane, although she claimed to be remiss in knowledge of her forebears, gave input during the first phases of my research. She was encouraging, saying "You show a surprising industry and skill in research..." I was surprised when she commented, "You know more about my antecedents than I do."

Like any family history, the Ingalls saga continues to increase. Laura Ingalls Wilder's "Little House" characters have become the stuff of history. Through Laura's storytelling, they have come to represent the great era of American pioneering.

I hope this *Story of the Ingalls Family* helps to answer questions for you, as my research on these historical figures did for me.

W.T.A
February 1993

Cover Photo: The Ingalls family in the early 1890s.
Seated: Ma, Pa, Mary; standing: Carrie, Laura, Grace.
(original at Laura Ingalls Wilder Home, Mansfield)

First edition.............March 1993		Seventh printing..............May 2000	
Second printing..........April 1994		Eighth printing..............April 2002	
Third printing............June 1995		Ninth printing................May 2004	
Fourth printing...........June 1996		Tenth printing................May 2006	
Fifth printing.........February 1998		Eleventh printing............May 2008	
Sixth printing...........March 1999			

*Illustration for Laura Ingalls Wilder's **Little House in the Big Woods** by Helen Sewell, from original Harper & Brothers edition.*

I. Meet the Ingalls Family

When Laura Ingalls Wilder published her first book, *Little House in the Big Woods* in 1932, she had no idea that she was creating a lasting fame for herself and her family. She wrote simply to preserve a tale of frontier life and to share with readers the ways of the pioneer. She also wrote to record her father's stories and his fiddle's songs. Her desire to pay tribute to Pa Ingalls resulted in a new career for herself as a writer and a widespread new family of readers.

Laura saw in her own life the rapid transition change from pioneer days to life in modern America. But she wanted readers to understand, as she said, "what is behind the things they see; what it is that made America." For generations, her own family had helped to make America. Her father, Charles Ingalls, could tell of his ancestors sailing from England to Massachusetts at the time of the Puritans. Her mother, Caroline Quiner, spoke of wealthy Scots ancestors in her background, who also settled in New England.

1

From those roots, the branches of Quiner and Ingalls families steadily ventured further west.

Charles Phillip Ingalls was born on January 10, 1836 in Cuba, New York, the third-born of Lansford and Laura Colby Ingalls. In 1842, the family moved west to Illinois. Then there were five children: Peter, Charles, Lydia Louisa, Polly and Lansford James. The Ingallses pioneered on the prairies west of Chicago before moving again to southeastern Wisconsin around 1851. Eventually there were four more children: Laura Ladocia, Hiram, George and Ruby.

Laura and Lansford Ingalls, parents of Pa; grandparents of Laura Ingalls Wilder.

The Ingalls family settled along the Oconomowoc River near the village of Concord. Charles and his brothers worked alongside their father in carving a home from the forests; the Ingalls boys learned to be expert woodsmen, hunters, trappers, builders and farmers. And Charles developed a skill that made him popular in the neighborhood: he learned to play the fiddle. No one recalls how, but he acquired his own violin during the 1850s.

Living near the Ingallses were the Quiners. Henry and Charlotte Tucker Quiner had arrived in the wilderness region just west of Milwaukee in 1839. (Their family origins were Massachusetts and Connecticut). They brought with them three children: Martha, Joseph and Henry. On December 12, 1839 another daughter was born, Caroline Lake. She became the mother of Laura Ingalls Wilder, the "Ma" of the "Little House" books.

Henry Quiner was a trader with the Wisconsin Indians in addition to farming land on the old territory road near Battle Town Creek. Indians were frequent visitors to the Quiner cabin, and the children grew used to seeing them. Two more Quiners were added to the family in Wisconsin: Eliza and Thomas.

Tragedy struck the Quiners in the fall of 1844. Father Quiner sailed with his brother-in-law Mc Gregor on a trading trip to the straits of Mackinaw. An autumn storm sunk the schooner and all but one was lost. Charlotte Quiner was left alone in the wilderness with five children between the ages of ten and two. Thomas was born a month after his father died.

"Hard times" was the way the Quiner children remembered life after their father's death. Indians helped feed the family, and often when food was low, kindly neighbors appeared from the forest with needed supplies for them.

"Mother went through the hardship of a pioneer life," recalled her daughter Martha. Charlotte Quiner sold the family's original land claim and moved her children to a forty acre tract of government land near Concord in 1848. The following year, she married a Connecticut farmer, Frederick Holbrook. They had one child, Charlotte, called Lottie.

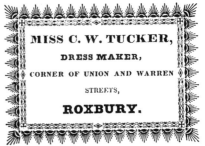

Advertisement (circa 1830) of Charlotte Tucker of Boston, mother of Caroline, grandmother of Laura Ingalls Wilder.

As neighbors, the Quiner-Holbrooks and the Ingallses shared lives of pioneer farming, but there was time for picnicking, skating on the Oconomowoc, spelling schools, church and dances. Three marriages occurred between the families. Polly Ingalls married Henry Quiner, Charles Ingalls married Caroline Quiner and Peter Ingalls married Eliza Quiner.

After their marriage on February 1, 1860, Charles and Caroline farmed near Concord. Caroline had taught school before her marriage and loved books and writing. In her clear, precise handwriting she reported news of herself and her husband in an 1862 letter to her sister Martha:

And now about Charles and Caroline. We are well and enjoying ourselves. You will think I am healthy when I tell you how much I weigh. I weigh 138 pounds. Charles is well but has worked hard this summer and is about tired out now. We have our hops picked and pressed. It took three weeks and 20 pickers to pick them . . .

Charles and Caroline's photo must have been taken soon after their 1860 wedding. (Original at Laura Ingalls Wilder Home, Mansfield, Missouri)

Both Charles and Caroline Ingalls were hard workers. And, as their daughter Laura later said, "They possessed the spirit of the frontier to a marked degree."

The Civil War was raging in 1862 when Lansford and Laura Ingalls and most of their children moved again, this time north to the "Big Woods" of Pepin County. The village of Pepin was built along the shore of Lake Pepin, a widened extension of the Mississippi River.

In 1863, Charles and Caroline and Henry and Polly followed their relatives into the Big Woods. The two couples bought a farm seven miles from Pepin. This became the scene of *Little House in the Big Woods.* There the first two Ingalls children were born: Mary Amelia on January 10, 1865 and Laura Elizabeth on February 7, 1867.

Charles and Caroline were now Pa and Ma.

"Our little family must be self-sufficient for its livelihood," said Laura of the Wisconsin life she first knew. Pa hunted, trapped, farmed, fished, and worked at carpentry, a skill he had developed for a lifetime. He was also a responsible citizen in the developing neighborhood. His name appears on election rolls, as treasurer of the nearby Barry Corner School and on other public records.

Ma was a thrifty, creative pioneer wife and mother. She was also a cultured woman who had educated herself well, despite the difficulties of her girlhood. Mary and Laura were soothed by Ma's gentle voice reading aloud to them from the books and papers she cherished, as much as they were by Pa's fiddle music.

Life was comfortable in the Ingalls cabin in the Wisconsin woods. But Charles Ingalls longed for the open prairies. He wanted to go west.

II. Ten Years of Travel

In 1868, Charles and Caroline Ingalls sold their Wisconsin farm; the following year they journeyed to land they had purchased near Keytesville, Missouri. This move represented the start of their long search for a productive farm and a permanent home in the west. It took ten years of frequent moves, hard luck, hard work and adventures for the Ingalls family to finally achieve what Ma wanted so much: a home. Most of their experiences were told by Laura Ingalls Wilder in the "Little House" books.

The Missouri interlude was very short for the Ingalls family. They moved on to Montgomery County, Kansas, where they were living on the prairie thirteen miles from the town of Independence in 1870. These times Laura described in *Little House on the Prairie*, a book she wrote from family stories, her own faint memories and a little research.

The land on which Pa built a cabin was actually Indian Territory, a reserve promised by the government for the Osage tribe. Indians were frequent sights for Laura and Mary; although she'd grown up with them herself, Ma was often frightened by the Osages.

In the cabin on the prairie, the third daughter was born, Caroline Celestia, called Carrie. The family Bible recorded the day as August 3, 1870.

While Pa and Ma labored to build a new home and farm on the Kansas prairie, the Osage Indians resented such intrusions by the settlers. Tensions grew between the tribes and the pioneers; rumors suggested that the whites would be driven away.

But finally an agreement was made; the Indians were paid, and they rode off, again pushed further west.

For the Ingalls family, another move beckoned. They were not going west, but home to Wisconsin. The buyer of the Pepin farm had not paid for it and its ownership returned to Pa. Again, they made the long covered wagon trip, but this time north.

The Ingalls were settled again in their little house in the woods by the spring of 1871. They picked up life as it has been before the Kansas move, and Pa farmed his Pepin land for two more years. He still wanted to move west, so in October, 1873, the farm was sold a second time.

During the 1870's, Pa and Ma's names appeared on many documents of land sales, deeds and property exchanges . . .

Charles P. Ingalls

Caroline L. Ingalls

The Ingalls family crossed the Mississippi and drove straight west across Minnesota. As told in *On the Banks of Plum Creek,* they stopped along Plum Creek, near Walnut Grove, Minnesota. Their first home was a dugout and Laura's writings describe life there and in a later frame house from 1874-1875.

Life near Walnut Grove included many Norwegian neighbors, like the Nelsons, and the experience of regular school and church activities for Mary and Laura. Pa's goal was to become a successful wheat farmer, but his plans were thwarted by the grasshopper years of the mid-1870s. Twice he was forced to leave his family and travel to eastern Minnesota to work for wages as a harvester.

Plum Creek, Walnut Grove, Minnesota.

After his return in the fall of 1875, the only Ingalls son was born. He was Charles Frederick and the date was November 1, 1875.

Successive crop failures in Walnut Grove forced Pa and Ma to again disrupt their goal of farming in the west. During the summer of 1876, they sold the Plum Creek property and agreed to help friends operate a hotel in Burr Oak, Iowa. On the way to Iowa, the family stopped for an extended stay with Peter and Eliza Ingalls and their children along the Zumbro River. While there, nine-month old Charles Frederick died on August 27, 1876. He was buried in South Troy, and mournfully his family continued on to their new life in Iowa.

The town of Burr Oak, Iowa was at a crossroads of east and west travel. The Burr Oak House, the hotel Pa and Ma helped manage, was a busy place, full of boarders, travelers and those who stopped for a hot meal. For a while, the hotel was a home for the Ingalls family, but they left for rented quarters elsewhere as soon as they could. Being very private people and particular in

6

their children's rearing, Pa and Ma did not want Mary, Laura and Carrie exposed to strangers and events like the one Laura always remembered: the drunken man shooting a hole in the kitchen door while pursuing his wife.

The hotel in Burr Oak, Iowa, where the Ingalls family lived in 1876.

Pa worked as a carpenter, as a millwright and at anything he could, but the Ingallses were very poor in Burr Oak. The girls all attended the town's redbrick school where they were outstanding scholars, and the family was active in the Congregational Church. But Burr Oak was not a destination but a stopping place.*

Laura did not write of the three years which elapsed between her books *On the Banks of Plum Creek* and *By the Shores of Silver Lake* in her "Little House" series. Turning east did not fit her tale of a family moving west, and Burr Oak was not a typical frontier town. As Laura explained, her books included stories as she remembered living them, but she did not write her entire life story.

As to the poverty and difficulties her family suffered, Laura explained their amazing courage and strength as typical of the times. She and Mary knew of hardships, but as Laura said, "someway were shielded from the full terror of them . . . The spirit of the frontier was one of humor and cheerfulness no matter what happened. My parents refused to dwell on hardship but looked ahead to better things."

The fourth daughter and last child of the Ingalls family was born while they were living in a rented brick house in Burr Oak. The Ingalls Family Bible recorded the birth of Grace Pearl Ingalls on May 23, 1877. Mary was then twelve, Laura, ten, and Carrie, almost seven.

After Grace's birth, Pa's intense desire to return to the western prairies again gnawed at him. His fiddle played roaming songs, moving tunes and restless music. Ma joked that all Pa had was an

---

*For more details on the Burr Oak experiences, see Laura Ingalls Wilder: The Iowa Story, by William Anderson (1990).

Helen Sewell illustration from original Harper & Brothers edition of **On the Banks of Plum Creek.**

itchy foot, but she too knew the meaning of the saying, "It is better, farther on." Laura recalled that Pa and Ma always discussed their plans together, and late in 1877, they agreed to return to Walnut Grove.

When they completed the covered wagon trip back across Minnesota, the Ingalls family stopped right in the village of Walnut Grove. They spent 1878-1879 not as farmers, but as townspeople. Pa built them a little house and since the town was growing, he often worked at carpentry. He also opened a butcher shop briefly, did jobs of all sorts for daily earnings, and was elected as Justice of the Peace when the town government got organized in the spring of 1879.*

Laura's *By the Shores of Silver Lake* mentions briefly the sorry tragedy suffered by her family early in 1879. It was Mary's blindness. "Brain fever" was the official cause of Mary's loss of sight; in those days the term could cover many diseases. Although Pa and Ma sought the best medical help available, Mary's eyesight dwindled to the day when the bright blue of Grace's eyes was the last she saw. She was fourteen.

For a decade, Charles and Caroline Ingalls had sought a permanent homestead without success. Pa's wanderlust almost lured his family clear to the Pacific coast; a friend of his urged him to move to Oregon. But Ma was concerned about an education for her growing girls and finding opportunities for blind Mary. She compromised with Pa: one more move, west to Dakota Territory.

---

*For more about the Ingalls family's life in Minnesota, see *The Walnut Grove Story of Laura Ingalls Wilder,* by William Anderson (1987).

Travels of the Ingalls Family

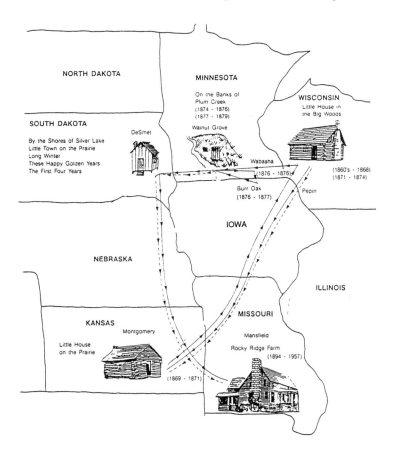

From her birthplace in Wisconsin to her final home in Missouri, Laura Ingalls Wilder's pioneering journeys with her family are traced.

III. Dakota Territory:
Railroading and Homesteading

I n 1879, the Chicago and Northwestern Railroad Company was expanding its tracks from western Minnesota into Dakota Territory. The rolling Dakota prairies were opening up to homesteaders and railroad service and new towns needed developing in the territory. Pa saw the quarter sections (160 acres) of free government homestead land as a way to resume farming in the west. But getting started was costly; Pa had little money to invest in new buildings, tools and seeds on vacant homestead land. To stake himself, Pa again used his varied talents: he took a clerical job with the railroad camps as the tracks were being laid through the townsites of Brookings and De Smet, Dakota Territory.

Fortunately, Pa and Ma raised each of their children to enjoy reading and to excel in writing a good story as well as telling one. Fifty years after the Ingalls family moved to Dakota, Carrie recorded her memories of the first year spent in De Smet . . .

Father and Mother, Mr. and Mrs. C.P. Ingalls with their family, Mary, Laura, Grace and myself came to the C&N.W.-R.R. construction camp on the banks of Silver Lake in 1879 where father was timekeeper, bookkeeper and paymaster. This was the stretch of the R.R. grading from Brookings to De Smet. Trains came only to Tracy, Minn. From there we had to come overland in a spring buggy.

It was an ideal place for a camp for Silver Lake was a beautiful little lake full of water. This was

Charles and Caroline Ingalls

10

probably why the Surveyor's House was built on its bank.
I do not know anything about the working of the
grading only it was done with horses and scrapers. I was
not allowed to go far and never where the work was being
done.

At night there would be a cloud of dust and the shout-
ing men and trotting horses toward camp from work,
which was the understood signal for me to go in. Then
supper and bed.

But I do know there were some fine horses on the work,
every man proud of his team, and often I remember
father saying a good deal of rivalry about a team's ability,
their knowledge of how to pull a scraper not to delay the
line, and when the dump was coming and the style and
grooming of the horses. It was no wonder that sometimes
a horse thief picked a team. Sometimes a lone horseman
would come out of the prairie, ride up and watch the
grading work and ride away again into the prairie
spaces, as they say, and that night the men would sleep
with their teams.

One such horseman, wearing always a red shirt, big
hat, and light trousers, and riding a white horse, not such
a beautiful horse, but father remarked once "a mighty
good one," when this horseman took a fancy to a horse or
team they were just the same as gone, for he had the
courage of his convictions and the nerve of a - - - -, but I
really don't know what a good horse thief has the courage
of. I saw him riding through many times and to me he was
great, but fearsome. There were many little things like this
to make an impression on one's memory.

In the fall of 1879 when it was too late for the R.R.
grading work the camp broke up and the surveyors went
away, but as they were to come back in the spring. They
persuaded father and mother to stay and move into their
house* for the winter where they could leave the survey-
ing outfit.

Father purchased their food supply which was quite a
quantity, the only item I remembered was a large barrel

---

*The Surveyors' House was purchased by the Laura Ingalls Wilder Memorial
Society, Inc., of De Smet, South Dakota in 1967. It has been restored and is
open to the public.

with just about two layers of "hard tack" in the bottom which they said was not enough to count and I had my first and last taste of genuine hard tack, memory has it that it was delicious.

Mr. R.A. Boast put up a house just a very little way, could not have been more than a hundred feet north of us; then brought Mrs. Boast there.

The folks often said the winter was

Carrie, Mary, and Laura

mild, but I cannot recall about the snow or cold, I know we were all very comfortable. We two families spending the most of our evenings together. I used to go to sleep listening to father play songs, dance music, and hymns on his old violin or to the singing of hymns from that old "Pure Gold" hymn book which we all knew by heart before spring. It seemed a very happy time to me and looking back I know it must have been for the lifelong friendship of the Boast and Ingalls families proved it.

Sometimes there were men traveling through and they always seemed so glad of a place to stop and always seemed to give the impression of coming from a long way off.

Mr. Boast often told of entertaining the people of De Smet and Lake Preston, for New Year's dinner. That was our family and a man who had taken a claim at Lake Preston but was staying at our house, nine in all.

That was a lovely day, we ate dinner with the door open and after I had eaten all I could I left the others talking at the table and went out to play.

It did not seem to get cold again and more men traveled through. And a preacher came and held church services at our house. It seemed an awful long service, so long to just sit still. That date was February 2nd, 1880. That is what father and mother always said and Mary later told me. The preacher was Rev. Alden a home missionary from Minn., who came many times afterward.

As it got warmer the wild ducks and geese began to come, I remember early one morning there was such a noise, a din, it would be called, I ran out to see what it was. The lake was covered with wild geese, they were swimming and splashing and there were little waves on the lake, and every goose was talking. I was told they were choosing their mates for it was Valentine's Day and it was said birds chose their mates that day. That is how I remember the date. Mornings I used to watch the lake and with the wind blowing the water in little waves and the wild ducks and geese and quite a few times beautiful swans on its water it was a sight no child could forget.

Spring came and with it the surveyors. Father used to go with them and one day he came home and said the town was all located. So after dinner I went to the top of the hill east of where the court house is now to see the "town" and all I saw was a lot of stakes in the ground. I went back and told mother there was nothing but sticks stuck in the ground and mother told me that where the stakes were would be houses and stores, a school house and a church.

Then in a little while we moved "to town," father putting up the house E.H. Couse bought for his first store. Then father built a house on the corner (this was the store building used as a residence by the Ingalls during the Hard Winter and during several later winters—Author's note) that Carroll bought for his bank. This house was moved back quite a while later and is now C.L. Dawley's real estate office. My father, C.P. Ingalls was first justice of the peace in Kingsbury County and the first justice court was held in the front room of our home.

Church services were also held there until the depot was put up, then the services were held there. Benches were made of boards, I certainly remember that. At that time there was just one other little girl my size in town . . .

There was great joy and thoughtfulness and the lives of those early pioneers were bound together in an effort to build for the future not only a town, but a good town.

IV. Settling Down in De Smet

As first citizens of De Smet, the Ingalls family knew that they were a part of history. They kept notes on early developments; Ma wrote about the founding of the Congregational church and Pa recorded the formation of the county and the town.

"I made a trip to Brookings in February," Pa wrote, "and took a homestead. The N.E. 1/4 section, township 110, range 56." That land became the Ingalls farm, where they lived from 1880-1887.

Pa bought town lots in De Smet early in 1880. He constructed two buildings, sold one and kept the "store" at Main and Second Streets. There, in May, 1880, De Smet's first child was born. He was Arthur Kingsbury Masters, the son of friends from Walnut Grove who had also moved to Dakota. After the first summer and fall on the homestead, the Ingalls family moved back into Pa's store building to endure the "Hard Winter" of 1880-1881. It is told in Laura's book *The Long Winter*. For the next several years they returned to De Smet for the winter, fearing the possibility of being blizzard-bound on the homestead. While Laura and Carrie and Grace enrolled in De Smet's early school, blind Mary was absent from home, attending the Iowa College for the Blind at Vinton. Pa and Ma enrolled her in November of 1881 and she began a seven year course in academic and manual training. Dakota Territory had no provision for education of the sightless and had an agreement with Iowa for making the school at Vinton available for students like Mary.

Mary

Although her family missed her during the seven years she studied in Iowa, they all were proud of her progress and pleased with her opportunities for study and socialization. Among Mary's course work was Arithmetic, U.S. History, Physiology, Natural History, Chemistry,

14

Rhetoric, Literature, Political Economy, Algebra and General History. She excelled in music: vocal, harmony, piano and organ. Manual training for the blind was stressed in Vinton and Mary learned to sew, knit, tie horse fly nets, make rugs and hammocks and other "fancy work". When she came home for summer vacations she amazed family and friends with examples of intricate beadwork.

While Mary completed her education, Laura taught three terms of school near De Smet. Her own school days ended when she married Almanzo Wilder on August 25, 1885. They farmed a homestead and a tree claim north of De Smet. There the only Ingalls grandchild was born on December 5, 1886 and named Rose Wilder.*

Some of Mary's beadwork

In 1885 Pa sold his Main Street store building to Judge John Carroll for $600. The building was moved to the back of the lot to make way for a grand brick bank building. It was still standing in 1912 when it was photographed. Later it was dismantled and the lumber used to build a house in town.

Pa's store building in De Smet.

From 1885-1887, the Ingalls family lived on the homestead, but the onset of dry years discouraged farming. Finally, Pa and Ma decided to become permanent De Smet residents. Ma owned two lots on Third Street in the growing residential district of De Smet; on one of them Pa constructed a house during the fall of 1887. On Christmas Eve they moved in. At first, the house was small: two rooms on the first floor with a large attic overhead. The little house on Third Street was journey's end for Charles and Caroline Ingalls. They never moved again.

Pa enlarged his house over the years; a low-ceilinged kitchen was added and a parlor and three bedrooms made it no longer

---

* Like Pa and Ma, Laura and Almanzo lost an infant son in 1889.

little. Downstairs was the parlor, dining room, kitchen, Mary's bedroom and the parents' bedroom. Narrow, twisting stairs led to three sleeping rooms upstairs for Carrie and Grace and boarders who sometimes came and went.

Ingalls home in winter.

The Third Street house was sided and painted a soft gray. Pa laid a flat open porch in front and planted shade trees all around. A sandpoint pump outside the kitchen door was the water supply. Rails and clothes lines were guides for Mary around the yard. The barn and out house stood next to the alley. Most of the backyard was filled with a big garden. Wild plum thickets and apple trees grew outside the kitchen windows.

The Ingalls home was a pleasant, cozy place. Wallpaper covered the walls and the floors were covered with lengths of rag carpeting sewn by Mary. Lace curtains and houseplants were at the tall paned windows. Pa built a convenient kitchen cabinet of drawers and shelves in the kitchen where the sink and cookstove were set up. A fancy nickel-plated hard coal heater stood sentinel in the parlor and its steady heat radiated through most of the house.

On December 20, 1888, Charles Ingalls "proved up" on his homestead claim and received his "patent" (land title) from the government. But he no longer farmed. For Pa, the goal of being an independent farmer in the west was never realized. Poor farming conditions and the drought years of the late 1880s and early 1890s signaled the end of an unfulfilled dream. In 1892, the farm was sold for $1200.

After moving to De Smet, Charles Ingalls became the town carpenter. He was called on to work at house-building and repairs in town and country. A neighbor girl recalled Pa's comings and goings, mentioning that "Often have I seen Mr. Ingalls carrying his tool box up the back way from his carpentry work; tall and spare with intense blue eyes and a dark, rather long mustache." Aubrey Sherwood, a neighbor boy, remembered Pa's "flowing beard, dressed on work days with tools on his belt."

The pioneer days were done; the Ingallses were townspeople.

❖

V. A Family on Third Street

Mary Ingalls graduated from the Iowa College for the Blind on June 12, 1889, when she was 24. At commencement exercises on June 10 she read a Robert Burns essay, "Bide a Wee and Dinna Weary," which, as Laura said, "showed the influence of Pa's old Scots songs. After graduation, she returned to De Smet to live at home. She never regained her sight and never married.

For Mary Ingalls, life became a procession of days filled with housework, music of the parlor organ, church, craftwork and visiting with friends who stopped in. She moved around the house with ease. Strangers seldom sensed that she was blind; her blue eyes were only slightly vague. She helped Ma with housework, sewing and cooking. Her days had a set routine: housework in the mornings and afternoons in the parlor filled with reading, writing and crafts.

Mary wrote many letters to family and college friends, using her Braille slate and stylus or penciling letters with the guidance of a wide grooved insert on the slate. She had a library of Braille and raised print books and read widely from them.

Ma and her sisters read aloud everything that came into the house, so Mary did not lack for news and knowledge.

For years, Mary composed poetry, with themes of patriotism, religion and home. She wrote an affectionate ode to Pa and his fiddle, mentioning that:

And oft when daily toil was done
The household gathered one by one
The happy blue eyed sisters four
'Ere yet stern fate had taught them more
Than the alphabet of worldly lore
The mother to wrest from the day 'ere its close
One restful hour of sweet repose
The father from toilsome day respite to win
And solace find in his violin . . .

Mary's health was sometimes a family concern and in July of 1892 she and Pa made a trip to Chicago to consult with eye specialists. They were told that nerve damage would never allow Mary's sight to return, but a delicate operation was performed to relieve severe neuralgia pains in the head and face. When asked about Mary's sight years later, Laura mentioned that all that could be done for her blind sister had been done.

While Ma and Mary ran the household, Carrie and Grace were busy with school. The 1884 school building was two blocks west of the Ingalls home and there the two youngest Ingalls daughters finished their educations. When Carrie finished high school she taught briefly and then learned the printing trade at *The De Smet News and*

Third Street, showing three windows of Ingalls house.

Leader. Hers was a long working career alternating between printing, clerking in stores, helping in the Post Office and other occupations. Her wages were welcome at home, for the Ingalls family was never prosperous.

Grace was sometimes known as "Gracie" at school. She, along with Mary and Carrie, was involved in Sunday School and the young people's league at the Congregational Church around the corner from their home.

The Ingalls family were well-known in the neighborhood and at church, but one neighbor recalled that they "kept to themselves." They lived quietly, with much of their attention centering on Mary and old friends like the Boasts. Ella Boast suffered with severe arthritis so her husband gave up their farm to move to De Smet. Though very crippled, Mrs. Boast directed her hired girls to prepare bountiful holiday dinners and other celebrations and the Ingalls family was often present.

When a Masonic order was started in De Smet, Pa became an active member. In 1892, Bethlehem Chapter of the Order of Eastern Star was formed and both Ma and Carrie were charter members. Pa soon joined the Eastern Star along with them.

It was Pa who was most active in De Smet's community life. He held many civic jobs, some of them paying small fees which supplemented his carpentry business. He was town clerk, deputy sheriff, street commissioner, chief of police and for several years was justice of the peace. As justice, Pa served papers on cases including assault, intent to kill, and illegal sale of liquor. He was personally a prohibitionist and *The De Smet News and Leader* mentioned in 1890 one of the cases he handled as justice: "Drink loves a shining mark, but C.P. Ingalls seems in duty bound to exert the 'powers that in him lie' to redeem the fallen and bring to justice those who willfully violate the prohibitionary law."

Pa may have sold insurance and is said to have canvassed the county taking orders for twine farmers needed to bind their grain. In 1892 he decided to start his own store. It was called "Ingalls and Company" and had several locations in downtown De Smet. The

Pa, circa 1894

store featured groceries, variety goods, tinware, school supplies and "notions." Mary's fancy fly nets for horses were on sale as well as harnesses and halters.

The store was short-lived. The drought years of the 1890s

Ma in 1897

slowed farming and business all through South Dakota (the territory became a state in 1889). Pa's store was no match for larger concerns like the Loftus or Harthorne's operations. "Ingalls and Company" closed out after a year and Pa started traveling across the prairies with a grocery wagon. He stopped at isolated farms selling his goods to farm wives who seldom got to town.

The drought of the '90s led Laura and Almanzo Wilder to leave De Smet in 1894, taking their daughter Rose and all their remaining possessions to a new farm at Mansfield, Missouri. Pa and Ma, Mary, Carrie and Grace all stood around the house on Third Street to bid them farewell. It was the first permanent separation within the family. It was the last time any of the family saw little Rose.

Ma was pleased that three of her girls taught school, carrying

19

on the tradition that stretched back to their grandmother Charlotte Quiner. Grace prepared for her teaching career at Redfield College, a small Congregational school west of De Smet. She took a "normal course", which was common preparation for teachers of that era. For Grace, the late 1890s were busy as she finished her schooling and then taught in country schools.

While Grace taught the Lincoln School on the prairie near Manchester (a small town seven miles west of De Smet), she met pioneer

Carrie

families like the Dunns, the Aspinwalls and the Dows. Soon Nate Dow was courting her. He was the son of a homesteader and farmed the family land near Manchester. On October 16, 1901 Grace and Nate were married at the Ingalls home. The groom was 42; the bride, 24. They settled in on the Dow farm.

Grace

Pa's health worried them all that fall of 1901. His heart was failing him and through the winter and spring of 1902 he became seriously ill. Grace often came in from her new farm home to help, but Pa grew no better. They sent for Laura, who made the train trip from Mansfield to De Smet. She arrived in time to see Pa again. But on Sunday afternoon, June 8, 1902, with his family around him, Charles Ingalls died.

Pa Ingalls, De Smet's first citizen, was buried on the prairie hill near town. "Charles Ingalls did his life's work well . . ." said *The De Smet News*. "As a friend and neighbor he was always kind and courteous and as a husband and father he was faithful and loving. And what better can be said of any man?"

VI. "Jogging Along in the Same Old Ruts"

After Pa's death, Ma, Mary and Carrie lived on together in the house on Third Street. Ma capably managed her slim finances and Carrie worked steadily as a store clerk or at newspapering. Their garden provided food, and rent money paid for other expenses. Usually, renters filled the spare rooms of the house.

Soon after Pa died a lifelong friendship was forged with a young couple who rented the upstairs of the Ingalls home. They were Ernest and Minnie Green, who moved to De Smet from Iowa. Lawyer Green was busy all day long in his office downtown, so Minnie spent her time with Mrs. Ingalls and Mary. They had much in common. When the Greens built their own home and moved, the friendship continued. Their three children grew up knowing Ma as their "Grandma Ingalls."

Kind neighbors helped Ma and her daughters in many ways, often stopping in to visit or bringing a loaf of bread or a glass of jelly. Living across the alley was the Henry Hinz family, with their eight children. For years, they brought a fresh pail of milk each evening for the Ingalls ladies.

Two of the Hinz girls, Marion and Lillian, grew especially acquainted with Ma and Mary. They brought their mail from the post office, took Mary walking, ran errands or sat visiting in the parlor. Mary was an interesting character to neighborhood children, being the only blind lady in town. Most children knew Mary from seeing her on the porch where she sat in her rocking chair on fine days. Marion and Lillian knew her better; they heard her read aloud from Braille, saw her string beads from memory and listened to her tell stories.

Another neighbor child recalled visiting Mary as she sat in her tall-backed reed rocking chair "The shades were drawn, her blue eyes wide open but sightless. I have heard that she could distinguish light and dark and that the light bothered her. The parlor was plainly furnished but neat, with Mrs. Ingalls bustling around. She was a short person, not thin, but very pale from staying so much inside I thought. Her life seemed to revolve around Mary."

The Congregational Church was very important in the lives of Ma and her daughters. Both Ma and Mary played the organ for services and on Sunday mornings they emerged from the front door to walk around the corner to church. Usually they wore long black dresses or skirts, with white blouses, and always they wore their gloves and black hats. When they walked, Mary just touched her mother's elbow for guidance. They were very proper ladies, but also very gentle and kindly.

Ma and Mary never traveled far from home; their longest journeys were to Grace and Nate's farm near Manchester. They never ventured to Mansfield to see Laura and Laura never saw them after her visit at the time of Pa's death. But Carrie often was on the move.

With her frugally saved wages, Carrie visited Ingalls relatives in Wisconsin and Minnesota. In 1903, she traveled to Mansfield to see Laura and Manly. From 1905-1907 she was away from home in search of a healthy climate to relieve respiratory problems. She lived in Boulder, Colorado for a year and then moved on to Wyoming. When she returned to De Smet, she was rejuvenated enough to take a homestead claim.

When large tracts of homestead land were opened for filing in western South Dakota, Carrie claimed land twenty miles north of Philip, at a place called Top Bar. She had a tar-papered shack moved to the claim, and started spending the required six months in residence in the desolate region. This process of alternating between her claim shanty and Ma's home continued until Carrie "proved up" in 1909.

Ma wrote: "Carrie's claim. She has an acre fenced sod coal house by shanty 10 x 12 feet boarded up a little in the ground."

Ma in the sitting room at home, circa 1905. This was the first picture Carrie took and developed with her box camera. The flaw through the center was a knife mark, made accidentally as Carrie processed her film. She probably used the large walk in closet upstairs for developing her photography.

After doing her stints on the homestead, Carrie took printing jobs for income. She was fully capable in all areas of printing; she was a full-fledged printer with duties ranging from melting lead into type, editing, writing, ad work, binding and publishing newspapers. Her skill landed her a job with E.L. Senn, an owner of numerous South Dakota papers. This position required much travel and she was usually away from De Smet from 1909-1912.

Ma and Mary missed Carrie when she was away. She was the liveliest and most talkative of the family and was very active in Eastern Star and church affairs. When she was gone, the Third Street house was quieter than usual. Ma and Mary went about their routines, more and more dependent on one another. As Ma explained, "We are jogging along in the same old ruts as always."

VII. Shared Feet, Shared Eyes

The Senn newspapers were printed mainly for the purpose of publishing legal notices, such as mining claims and homestead claim data. The papers opened for business, printed the paid ads until the demand ceased and then moved on to new territories. Carrie was involved in publishing several of these newspapers on the flats of western South Dakota and finally in the Black Hills.

E.L. Senn required that his employees be ardent Republicans and Prohibitionists, but Carrie could only meet the anti-drink rule. She was a life-long Democrat. Her work apparently kept her in the good graces of Mr. Senn for she capably produced the newspapers of Pedro and Roseland, and moved into the Black Hills to managed *The Keystone Recorder* and *The Hill City Star*.

While in Keystone in 1911, Carrie met her husband, David N. Swanzey. He was an old-time Black Hills pioneer, originally from a prominent St. Louis family. The beauty and peace of the Black Hills appealed to him when he first saw the area while a salesman for the Round Oak Stove Company. Dave Swanzey was intrigued by the rich mining industry and became a prospector and owner of gold mines and other property in Keystone.

Carrie was a spinster past forty when she was befriended by kindly, courtly Mr. Swanzey in Keystone. He was a widower in his fifties, with two small children who needed a mother. When Carrie finished her work in Keystone and moved on to manage the nearby *Hill City Star*, Dave Swanzey still came courting.

Carrie and Dave were married in Rapid City on August 1, 1912. Carrie plunged into housekeeping and motherhood with the Swanzeys. The children, Mary and Harold, were eight and six, when Carrie became their mother. They

Carrie and step-children Mary and Harold.

responded immediately to Carrie's warm affection and jolly presence. Harold was in poor health, hard of hearing and in need of attention. Carrie dedicated much of her energy to his recovery.

At 42, after years of "paddling her own canoe", Carrie enthusiastically and lovingly began a new life among the towering rocks and pines of the Black Hills.

Ma and Mary and their friends were all surprised at Carrie's marriage, missing her but rejoicing in her new life. Carrie periodically made extended visits to De Smet, but Grace increasingly assumed the role of caregiver for Ma and Mary when they needed her.

Grace and Nate Dow never had children. They operated their farm on the prairie near Manchester with the help of hired men, because of Nate's severe allergic and asthmatic conditions. He was a tall, strong man, but the pollen of growing crops and the dust of the hay field often left him gasping. In 1908 the Dows rented the farm and made a long trip to Oregon and the Pacific coast, in search of a climate more suited to Nate's needs. Nate's sister Chloe Fuller and her son Jack ac-

Grace and Nate Dow, at home — 1908.

companied them on the visit to their sister Elvira's home. Jack recalled that his Uncle Nate received little benefit from the change of climate.

All through their farming years, Nate and Grace sought a solution to the situation. At one point, they listed the farm for sale and planned to settle in Oregon, taking Ma and Mary with them. But finally, they simply retired to De Smet and moved to the Ingalls home.

Ma turned eighty in 1919, the year the Dows came to live in the west rooms of the Third Street house. Through the years of widowhood, she had rented rooms in the house to people for long and short periods. She and Mary together kept house, with help from Laura, Carrie and Grace. As Mary said, "I am feet for Ma and Ma is eyes for me."

Into the quiet lives of the Dows and the Ingallses came a surprising new interest—following the careers of Nate's nephew Harvey Dunn, and Grace's niece Rose Wilder Lane. Harvey left Manchester to become a famous illustrator of books and magazines like *The Saturday Evening Post.* Ma and Mary knew him and enjoyed the news of his growing importance as a nationally-known artist.

Rose was also famous, as a newspaperwoman, a world traveler, and an author. She corresponded with her De Smet relatives, sending them gifts and copies of her books, including *The Story of Art Smith, The Peaks of Shala* and *The Dancer of Shamahka. The De Smet News* reported Rose's career, and Ma shared news of her travels and publications with the Sherwoods for the pages of their paper. Mary remarked to Carrie that Rose was "the only famous person in our family."

Starting in 1911, Ma and Mary also read Laura Wilder's name in print. She wrote regularly for *The Missouri Ruralist* and other publications. Laura shared her manuscripts and stories with the family in De Smet. Sometimes, Laura mentioned her pioneering girlhood and her parents and sisters in her writing.

More cars and fewer horses passed along Third Street as the 1920s began, but inside the Ingalls house there was little change. Nate and Grace's Victrola was heard more often than Mary's organ, but coal stoves and kerosene lamps *Laura at her Mansfield home, around 1913.*
still heated and lit the house Pa built. Ma and Mary still walked together and read together and attended church. Ma took a lively interest when a new minister named O'Neill and his family came to serve the church in 1923.

26

Ma Ingalls, 1917

The O'Neill daughter, Lenna, was a high school girl when her family came to De Smet. She was sent to buy vegetables from the Ingalls garden. "I loved to go," Lenna said, "for Mrs. Ingalls was so gentle and friendly. I loved her. She urged me to stop in often, and I sort of settled into life in a new town with Ma as my confidante."

To the end of her life, Caroline Ingalls was cheerful, her interest in church, friends and neighbors keen. She lived on, past her eighty-fourth year, dying on Easter Sunday, April 20, 1924.

Mrs. C.P. Ingalls, Pioneer of County, Dies at 84

Kingsbury county lost one of its pioneer women in the death of Mrs. C.P. Ingalls at her home here Sunday. She and her husband came to this locality in 1879 and lived in a claim shanty on the north shore of Silver Lake before there was a De Smet.

The death was unexpected and followed an illness of but a short time, altho Mrs. Ingalls has been feeble all winter.

Caroline Quiner was born December 12, 1839, at Milwaukee, Wis., and died at 5 o'clock p.m. Easter Sunday, April 20, 1924, at the age of 84.

She was married to Charles Ingalls of Milwaukee Feb. 1, 1860, whose death occurred June 8, 1902.

Five children were born to this union. Mary Ingalls of De Smet; Laura Wilder of Mansfield, Mo.; Caroline Swanzey of Keystone, S.D.; Frederick Ingalls, who died in infancy, and Grace Dow of De Smet.

The family moved to De Smet in 1879 where they have since resided. In 1880 Mr. and Mrs. Ingalls helped organize the Congregational Church at De Smet and were faithful members of the organization to the end of their lives. Mrs. Ingalls was also an early member of the Eastern Star chapter of De Smet.

Besides the four daughters the deceased is survived by three sisters, and one granddaughter, Rose Wilder Lane.

Mrs. Ingalls was a good mother, a good neighbor, and a good friend. The last few years she had been unable to get around to see people very much or to attend church, but her interest has been with her neighbors, friends and church. It was a pleasure to go and visit her as she was always interested, bright and happy.

The De Smet News report of Ma's death.

27

VII. Ingalls History Becomes Legend

After Ma's death, the Dows lived on with Mary, but the old house was never as happy as it had been. Mary was lonely and never really recovered from the shock of losing Ma, despite having Grace nearby and the attention of friends. Carrie made visits to De Smet to help the situation and Laura and Rose investigated homes for the blind where Mary might live. Finally, in 1926, Mary went to visit Carrie in Keystone. She never returned to DeSmet.

Carrie made her sister welcome in her home and did all she could to make Mary happy. After a long stay, Carrie was helping her sister prepare for the trip home when Mary suffered a paralyzing stroke in the fall of 1927. For a year, Carrie faithfully nursed Mary. They spent time in a sanatarium and in the Rapid City hospital. At last they returned to Carrie's house in Keystone. Mary was so helpless that caring for her was a difficult job.

The Swanzey home (at right) in Keystone, late 1920s.

In October of 1928, Mary suffered a final stroke. She died on October 17, at the age of 63. Carrie accompanied Mary back to De Smet where funeral services were held from her beloved Congregational Church. She was buried next to Pa and Ma, the first break by death among the Ingalls daughters.

Nate and Grace left the Ingalls home to return to Manchester. Mary had willed the house to Carrie, so it was rented to a succession of families through the 1930s. The remainders of the Ingalls belongings were stored in an upstairs room.

Poor farm prices in the late 1920s and the Dust Bowl years of the 1930s brought hardship to the De Smet area and the state of South Dakota. Because their income depended on rent money from their farm, Grace and Nate sunk into poverty and never really escaped. Their health also declined, and they lived very simply in a rented house in Manchester.

In 1931, Laura and Almanzo drove their Buick from Mansfield to South Dakota. They found the prairies in the same grip of drought that they had left in 1894. They enjoyed their time with Grace and Nate, but noted how ill both of them seemed. For Laura, De Smet seemed full of ghosts. She missed Pa and Ma and Mary, and friends like the Boasts, very greatly.

Driving across South Dakota the Wilders spent several days in Keystone with Carrie and her family. They met Carrie's husband Dave and his son Harold and toured the mines and points of interest in the Black Hills. For Carrie, Laura's visit was a great boon to her spirits. She confided that she felt very much alone,

Grace Ingalls Dow

and depended on her memories for comfort. She was excited when Laura told her about her book, which would be published as *Little House in the Big Woods*.

In April of 1932, the first book in the Ingalls family saga was printed. When copies arrived in South Dakota for her sisters, Grace was ill in the Huron hospital; Carrie came to help and read the book aloud to them both. Grace was diagnosed as a severe diabetic, a disease that plagued her through her remaining years.

Carrie and Grace both thrilled at the story Laura wrote of their family, never dreaming that it was start of a classic series of books on pioneering.

Carrie and Grace were both historically-minded women, readers and writers. Both contributed accounts to the fiftieth anniversary edition of *The De Smet News* published in 1930. Grace had

29

previously been the Manchester news correspondent for the *News*. She resumed the job in the 1930s, reporting on neighborhood happenings. Carrie, of course, had honed her skill at writing while in the newspaper field.

Carrie and Grace enjoyed finding interesting historical data among Ma's papers, and they shared their findings with Laura. Laura sometimes relied on her sisters' memories while continuing "Little House" books. And it was Carrie who located the words for the song "Let the Hurricane Roar" which Rose used in her book of the same title.

"Quietly proud of her heritage" was the way a friend remembered Carrie in Keystone. Since her marriage, Carrie had become a leading citizen of the village at the foot of Mount Rushmore. She served the Congregational

Dave and Carrie Swanzey

Church and Sunday School. She was involved in club work and Democratic politics. She loved getting friends together for parties and socials, where she was a softspoken, kind spoken participant. It was known that Carrie Swanzey was the aunt of Rose Wilder Lane and the sister of Laura Ingalls Wilder, but she never stressed the connection, nor attracted attention to herself.

Masonic and Eastern Star work kept both Carrie and Dave involved. They held many offices in the lodges and their closest friends and associations were Masonic ones. Eventually, funds from the Swanzey estate helped to build the Masonic lodge in Keystone.

While Grace and Nate Dow eked through the Depression years with financial help from Harvey Dunn and others, the Swanzeys were better off. Dave was station agent for the Burlington Northern Railroad that still shipped ore from the Keystone mines. Over the years, though his mine property lay dormant, Dave purchased rental houses around town. It was Carrie's job to collect the few dollars in rent each month.

Although Keystone was in one of the richest mineral districts of the world, Dave Swanzey's "big hit" never materialized. When mining waned, the carving of Mount Rushmore with the heads of Washington, Jefferson, Lincoln and Roosevelt, kept Keystone from becoming a ghost town. The road to Rushmore led past the Swanzey house, and Carrie was very interested in the progress of the memorial. She loved having De Smet friends visit her, so she often enticed them with news of the exciting work of Gutzon Borglum and his crews.

Dave Swanzey is generally credited with giving the granite mountain the name "Rushmore". He was also among a group of Keystone citizens who escorted Borglum for his first look at the carving site. Harold, the Swanzey son, overcame his youthful ill health and grew to be a strong man. He was among the workers who helped carve the mountain.

Carrie adored Harold and was grief stricken when he was killed in an auto accident in 1936. By that time, Mary Swanzey had been married for fifteen years to Monroe Harris. She was a happy, outgoing red-head, who was educated at a private school in Sioux Falls. Eventually, she had a family of eleven surviving children. Difficulties of rearing them during the Depression and their sheer numbers somewhat distanced Carrie and Dave from the Harrises. They finally settled in Hill City.

In April of 1938, David Swanzey died at 84. Carrie was left with the income from her husband's property for her lifetime, but she was also burdened with the complex responsibilities of the mining claims. Dave owned the Big Hit and Sitting Bull Lode mining claims, and Carrie must pay taxes to hold them. Gold lay in those mines, but government regulations forbade its mining. When the Wilders visited Carrie a month after her husband's death, she appreciated Laura's gesture of paying the mine taxes.

As a widow, Carrie continued her interests. She loved to read, but lost interest in housekeeping. She walked to church and to Eastern Star activities. She made trips to Rapid City and to visit Grace and Nate. During the tourist season, she sat on her porch swing, marveling at the cars which drove past on their way to Mount Rushmore. The monument was completed in 1941.

In the fall of 1941, Carrie was called back to Manchester to care for Grace in her last illness. Grace died on November 10, 1941, at the age of 64. She was buried near the Ingalls family in De Smet, and Nate followed her three years later.

Carrie always was interested in the present, but her strong sense of nostalgia made her thrill at Laura's continuing series of "Little House" books. She eagerly answered her sister's questions about the times described in the books and offered her own memories. Carrie's personal favorite was *These Happy Golden Years.*

When *Golden Years* was published in 1943, Laura remarked that "Sister Carrie writes me that after she read the book it seemed she was back in those times and all that had happened since was a dream. I considered it a great tribute to the truth of the picture I had drawn." In flyleafs of Carrie's copies of "Little House" books were warm messages from Laura, including this one:

> *Thoughts of childhood bring*
> *Sweet memories of you*
> *For thoughts of home are sweet thoughts*
> *And love of home is true*

Increasingly, the happy memories of the Ingalls family lived only in the pages of Laura's books. In 1944, after keeping the family home in De Smet for so long, Carrie finally sold the property. That same year, she and Laura donated Pa's fiddle to the South Dakota State Historical Society in Pierre. Carrie hoped that a museum could be established in De Smet where Ingalls items could be displayed. "I believe," she wrote, "if a few things were offered the city would at once prepare the necessary cabinets to care for them."

In October of 1944, Carrie and Laura met for the last time. Carrie's train trip to Mansfield was exciting to her and she was a happy guest on the Wilders' Rocky Ridge Farm. She saw the Ozarks in their fall splendor and was impressed with the Wilders' beautiful country home.

Carrie saw what Laura already knew: that their family history had become a classic story of American pioneering. The "Little House" books had preserved for the future what Laura and Carrie both cherished from their past. On her last Mansfield visit, Carrie met the reader-friends who stopped to see Laura; she saw the piles of fan mail arriving daily. Her pride increased that she was a part of Laura's writings.

Carrie Ingalls Swanzey's own measure of accomplishment in her town on Keystone was recognized when she was 75. In the spring of 1946, Mount Aetna Eastern Star chapter presented Carrie with a fifty-year membership medal and certificate. It was

Carrie (front row center) at Eastern Star ceremony honoring her as a 50-year member.

noted that she had "always lived for Eastern Star work and what it meant to her." As always, Carrie was delighted with a gathering of friends and a party atmosphere. She seemed in her usual excellent health.

A week later, Carrie was suddenly taken sick at home. Friends took her to the Rapid City hospital where she died on June 2. Keystone mourned her and the telephone brought the sad news to Laura that her remaining sister was gone.

Carrie wanted burial with her family in De Smet. Her wish was honored, and on a beautiful summer evening, she joined Pa and Ma and Mary and Grace in the De Smet cemetery. Except for Laura, the pioneer family was together again.

Aubrey Sherwood of *The De Smet News* thoughtfully wrote Laura of the scene: "Our minister, Mr. George G. Bell, recalled her well. Standing there on the green cemetery hill overlooking the prairie, he spoke of her coming from greener areas farther east, living here on the open prairie and then going to the mountains, to return here for her resting place. It was . . . a beautiful occasion."

For Laura, it was now necessary to tell her inquiring readers that "I am the only one left of the Ingalls family." "It seems strange," she mused, "that of all the people I wrote about, I am so far as I know the only one left."

But Laura had accomplished her goal: to tell, in simple storytelling, the tale of the Ingalls family, and through them, the story of all pioneers.

33

APPENDIX I:
The Diary of Grace Ingalls

G race Ingalls was nine years old when she started writing a sporadic diary in a lined "Exercise Book". It covers the years 1887-1893. At the time she began, the Ingalls family was living on their homestead claim near De Smet. The diary recounts the family move to Third Street, and serves as almost a "Little House" sequel in the way it includes anecdotes of family and friends. To preserve the originality of the diary, it is printed exactly as Grace wrote it.

While Carrie was visiting Grace in 1939, the two sisters enjoyed the nostalgia of reading over the diary. Two years later, when Grace died, Carrie evidently gathered up Ingalls family keepsakes and took them to her home in Keystone. The diary was rediscovered among the papers of Carrie's stepdaughter, Mary, following her death in 1969.

It is published here for the first time.

Jan. 12th 1887. Tuesday 1887.

Cousins Lee and Ella* came to day with their baby Earl, they came with a covered wagon and a stove. I think Earl is real petty. He is just beginning to talk and say any thing you say. He thinks everything of Laura's baby and so do I. Thay stayed two weeks and then went away. Laura has a baby and it is just beginning to smile. It is eight weeks old, her name is Rose. O yes Counsin peter came with my cousin's too. and is staying here now.

Jan. 29th Saturday. It is blisserd to day, I am glad it is not a school day. I am in Miss Masters** room now, and I am glad.

Feb. 9th Wednesday. Today is a very warm day, only the wind blows quite hard from the South, it is thawing. I havent been to school for a week but Carrie has, she stayed up to Mrs. Masters,*** and went to school and in the eavning took care of the boys while Mrs. Masters went to an entertainment, Carrie went to it on

---

* Ella Ingalls Whiting was a daughter of Peter and Eliza Ingalls and a first cousin of Grace.

** Miss G. Elgetha Masters, later the mother of Aubrey Sherwood.

*** Probably Mrs. George Masters. One of her "boys" was born in the Ingalls home in De Smet in 1880, the town's first birth.

Saturday for 10 cts. Yesterday Mrs. Boast and Mr. came over with Mrs. Collins and her boy Mr. George Collins and Mr. Frank Peck. We had lot's of fun and after dinner Mr. Collins played on the violen and on his mouth organ, after he had got threw playing Carrie and I played on the organ thay went home in the eavning. Pa is Deputy sheriff now he went up town this morning for Mr. Fieldby's horses and cutter. Mr. Fieldby's away from town for something.

Sunday 20th March. Today is snowing and blowing but is warm. a little while ago the snow was nearly all gone. but now there is lots of it. Laura was over a week ago and put Rose in short dresses, Rose is a big fat baby now but just as pretty. we have been to school nearley all this week, if you stay out you loose your half holiday. I like to go to school. we have a new study it is Physiology. we have to right the things down in our copy book. Last Thursday Carrie an eleaven more girls went and had there picture taken Mr. Owen was among them. While they were there I was over to Carrie Risedorph's she had three dolls she let me play with the bigerst one. we had lots of fun.

March 26, 1887. Saturday.
    To day is quite cold but all the snow has gone off. Laura has not been here for two weeks nor we their. Pa has been sick for a long while we had the doctor and he has just got well. Yesterday was speaking days we all went up to Mr. Owen's room. When Annie Wright spoke she looked real pretty she was Pussy Willow and was fixed up to look like it. Leana Sturgeon spoke a piece about mousie, she spoke low at first but at the end of it she pumped up and threw her arms up with a squeake, a little boy who sat on the front seat jumped out in front he was so scared, one of Mr. Owen's boy's spoke An old Women that lived in a shoe. There was a dialogue where there was a black women she was Neva Whaley the piece was called the Irish love letter there was good many other funny pieces.

May 4th 1887. To day is warm but the wind's blowing. I have not been to school for three days on account of my sore throat. Mary came home the 28th of April. she missed the train at M* and had

---

*"M" is unidentified. Depending on Mary's route home from Vinton, Iowa, she could have been waylaid at Minneapolis, or possibly in Mitchell, Dakota Territory.

to stay all night their. she was tiret when she got home but is all right now. Laura was over to day but did not get out of the buggy. There was a blow storm here and blew the wagon box and broke it all to pieces.

July 23 thursday. It has just through raining we went down cellar too, the clouds looked so funny. My birthday was may 23 monday. I got the prettiest vase I ever saw, it's color was gold. then I got a birthday cake, it was frosted and had lemon drops on top. We had an exhibition here in the hall 18 saturday night. we went up saturday to practice. O dear what fune we had Carrie had an acted poem named Mary Garwin it spoke about it in the paper, Dolly Dutton and the house that jack built were so funie. George Wilmerth was to. Forth of July I went up and had lots of nice things to eat. the big girls had a lemonade stand. the money was to get an organ for the church. We have two new teachers. Profeser Gleason and Miss Dawley. Sunday Manley went over to Charley Lampsons and his barn and haystacks burnt up, a great many town folks went down there. Mrs. Eliott saw the boy's running down the hill ahold of each others coat tailes, then she saw the fire.

Thursday Sep. 1, 1887 To day is warm but it has rained all the week, so pa could not hay. We have had lots of fun eating plums but have only one tree of plums left. Peter came over and helped us eat some one Sunday. There is going to be a show here and they are to have lots of animals. Mary and I study history we have got to the duch collines.* School is to begin in about a week, and I have a new dress. Pa has a new indian poney, but he is as big as peat, his name is jim, he has not bin broke only to ride.

Sat Oct 9, 1887. The leaves are turning yellow I have been to school three weeks we have a new principal, and teacher. Mr. Gleason is the principal he is very nice, he has a wife and baby. Pa has commenced building a house so we will live in town this winter. Jim broke the buggie tung for pa so pa traded him off for another pony. He is a little one with long main and tail.

Monday. March 5. 1888. Today is warm but the ice is not melted. We live in town now in not a very large house but beter than the

---

*Possibly "Dutch colonies" in America

shanty. It has two rooms below and one overhead We came hear the night before Christmas and it was the only plesant day for a long while. I have been to school all winter and am still going to Miss Master's I study Arithmetic, Reading, Spelling, Geography and Language. Our school-room is very nice. There are six windows, four of which have dark brown curtains or shades, the seates and desks are cullered a rose culler or very dark brown sutaibel for one schollar to sittin, the room is ornimated with pictures some with frames and some not. I like Miss Master's better and better. Laura and Manly were sick with diptheria and are just getting over it so we have Rose here. She is the best girl I ever saw. She can now say a good many words such as gramma and grampa and bread and butter and cracker.

April 13" 1888

It has been a long while since I have written for it is spring and a very wet one. We have a storm calendar and there is a storm nearley every day marked on it. I lost a week of school because I had the scarlet fever but no one knew it but us. School was closed on account of diptheria in town one little boy died with it. Miss Masters took the chance of the vaction and went and got married to Mr. Sherwood.* Miss Masters is a great deal taller than he so they must look funny togeather. Rose can walk nicely now she is broad as she is long. Carrie made two little cradels out of egg shells and gave one to Rose and one to Fay Baker. Fay is a cute little girl she lives in uncle Tom's house.*

—May 5 Saturday 1888. I am in Miss Dawleys room and I like her better than I do Mrs Sherwood. Jessie Robinson boards with us now and we have lots of fun. We stuffed my old rag doll in Carries bed once and were asleep when she came to bed so we dident have any of the fun at all until morning.

April 8th 1889 Monday.

We are having an april shower today the first one of the season. It has been nearly a year since I wrote in this book and still am in Miss Dawleys room. There was a great wind storm last week, the dust was so thick the houses on the other side of the street could hardly be seen. The prairie got on fire and a great

*Carter P. Sherwood of The De Smet News & Leader
**Thomas Quiner owned a house near Ingalls home on Third Street. The house was constructed by Charles Ingalls for his brother-in-law, in 1885.

many people were burned out and some burned to death. I like Miss Dawley better than any of my other teachers.

Tuesday August 27th 1889.

A great many things have happened since I last wrote in this book. Laura's little baby boy only a month old died a little while ago, he looked just like Manly. Rose will be three years old next december she is large for her age with golden hair and large blue eyes. Last friday Manly's house caught fire and burned to the ground. The furniture in the front room and in the bed room and pantry was saved but nothing in the kitchen where the fire started. Laura had just built a fire in their stove went into the other room and shut the door so she could sweep when the noise of the fire startled her and on opening the door she saw the roof and side of the kitchen was on fire . . . help came soon but they could not save the house and only some of their old clothing was saved they stayed down here for a while and then went to keep house for Mr. Sheldon one of their neighbors taking a hired girl with them. We do not know who will teach our room next time. Florette Bonney was hired but she changed her mind and went to Yankton. Sam Small lectured here a little while ago he is a tall thin man with a black mustache. Since then there has been a regular temperance campagne. We had six lechres. Mr. Small, Mr. Bain, Mr. and Mrs. Evans and the "Texas Cyclone" a man by the name of Jordan and some others who are not worth mentioning. I liked to hear Mr. and Mrs. Evans best. Mrs. Evans was a very sweet singer. The "Texas Cyclone" was a negro, he was very expressiave and gave such illustrations. Sam Small was an excellent speaker, I did not like his voice very well. He remonded me of Mr. Lagrange.

Sunday Nov. 17, 1889.

To day is warm and bright. Laura was down last saturday. They expect to go to Spring Valley in the spring. I am so sorry. They built a two room shanty and are living in it now. We have a teacher in our room now, her name is Miss Hilton. She is very short and wears glasses. Mrs. Drake let Herbert go home with his aunt, her other little baby is the best baby I ever saw, he will go for hours without crying. Well; Carrie is down in the Leader office learning to set tipe she gets a dollar a week now but after while she will get more. O yes, we carried prohibition by a great majority. North Dakota and Washington did too, Montana did not though. Mr. Fielder is coming in a day or to, to organize a prohibition enforcement league in DeSmet. Mary Moody had a fit here day before yesterday she staid allnight and went home in the afternoon.

Jan 2" 1890. This is the second day of the new year and the first time I have written it. It seems not very long ago since I wrote 1889 for the first time and thought it looked so queer. We intended to celebrate this day by going to Mr. Boasts but it looked so stormy we did not. Christmas we had quite a good time. Mr. Boasts folks and Manlys folks were down. I got a lovly book it is Tenneson's Dora the cover looks like marble. Uncle Tom* sent Mary a white silk handkerchief and ma and pa a picture of their two children Helen and Lillian they are both pretty. Carrie got a crazy work pincushion. We went to the tree and saw nothing but dolls. Carrie gave me my book and I can not find out how much it cost but I will yet though.

Grace Ingalls

April 21st 1890.

To day the wind is blowing hard, how I wish it would rain, it hasn't rained for a long while and the ground is as dry as powder. Laura is going the first of May and that isn't such a great while, going with a covered wagon, and take their stock. Summer is comming soon spring is here already, and Italians and beggars are here too a little while ago one of them came along with cinnamon bear a great ugly looking brute for ten cents he would preform, Mrs. Brunnell paid half and pa the other. he danced, turned springs and everything else. The man sang when the bear danced. Mary has been sick for over two months she had the la Grippe, we had Dr. Hunter. School is out for the weeks vacation. Mr. Owen** is just the horridest thing that ever was. Minnie and

*Thomas Quiner, a brother of Caroline Ingalls.
**V.S.L. Owen, one of De Smet's most outstanding early educators.

39

I had to go in his room for whispering he didn't do anything though we had fun.

May 18. 1890.

To day is Sunday it has eather been raining or blowing all day. We got all ready to go up to Laura's but it looked so like a storm we did not. They are going to Minn. tuesday after next, going with a covered wagon and drive the stock they and Peter sold their flock of two hundred and twenty sheep to the butchers for five hundred dollars. They are going in a covered wagon Peter, Manly, Laura & Rose they will have it nice two a bed set up all the time in the wagon. Laura will have her pretty poney to ride on part of the time. This is a cold spring even now the last of may it is so cold we can not take the stove out of the front room. The plum trees are all in bloom they can be smelled half a mile away. I don't suppose we will get many plums the other folks from town will though. We have rented twenty acres of the farm to Floyd at a dollar an acre, and six to Smith, a man that lives east of our place, at the same price. Such dredful sandstorm as we have here they come up just as a rain storm and it blows, and blows, and blows, all the time. though it has rained some this spring.

August 17th 1890.

I went to church this morning and heard the rev. Trout preach I do not like him very well. Laura went a long time ago they are not at Spring Valley. O Carrie and my self went to a picnic at Lake Henry we had the three seated rig we went to pick grapes Drakes folks and Franks were the rest of the company we had two hammocks. Joe Grey was the only boy he was just full of fun and we sang all the way home and didn't get back til half past nine. I had the best time I ever had before we had piles of fun.

DeSmet. June 23—1891—Monday.

It has been ten months since I wrote in this and nothing of consequence has happened everything goes on just the same. The crops have failed year after year in this place and are likely to this year. Carry still works down in the Leader office. We are to have a new teacher in the spring Prof. Shannon. I guess Mr. Owen will leave here. A lot of us scholars went out to his house in the last day of school and had a surprise party on him. We gave him a gold pen Sam Dwight presented it we had some fun. I was fourteen years old the 23d of May.

August 17th. 1891.

This is the hottest month we have had yet 100 degrees in the shade sometimes. They are having teachers institute there are more teachers than ever before. The new teacher Grace Skinner is a little bit of a fat woman with red hair. Wilson had a consort the other day. I was in the tamborine drill and the choruses. Every one says the drill was lovly we 12 girls had to go through all sorts of motions and marching we had red caps and white dresses with big bouquets every thing went off nice and D. R. was pleased with us.

While Grace kept her diary, Pa kept a store.

Sep. 3d 1893.

An now sixteen years old. We still live in De Smet and Carrie works on the same paper as before. Laura & Manly went to Florida came back and now live in De Smet. Peter went to Florida married a girl down in that country. The Prof. is a man by the name of Ferell he is irish, our old Prof. Shannon went to Chicago & got married. I have not been well for almost a year have had Dr.'s Rice and Ensign. Mary went to Chicago last summer and had an operation for the neuralgia. Aunt Lillie and her two children, Aunt Eliza, and aunt Martha visited with us last summer.

41

APPENDIX II:
The Families of the "Little House" Books*

Some of the Lansford and Laura Ingalls family: Standing: James, George, Hiram. Seated: Lydia Louisa, Laura, Lansford, Ruby. Photo courtesy of Rex Phillips.

Lansford Whiting Ingalls (1812-1896) and **Laura Colby** (1810-1883) were married in 1832. (Grandparents of Laura Ingalls Wilder). Their children were:

Peter Riley (1833-1900), who married Eliza Quiner
An infant son, born and died in 1835
Charles Phillip Ingalls (1836-1902), who married
    Caroline Quiner
Lydia Louisa (1838-1915) who married Isaiah Clough;
    later Joseph Stouff
Polly Melona (1840-1886), who married Henry Quiner
Lansford James (1842-1928), who married
    Sarah Dickinson
Laura Ladocia (1845-1918), who married
    L.D. Waldvogel; later Hiram Forbes
Hiram Lemuel (1848 - ?), who married
    Elizabeth Forbes
George Whiting (1851-1901), who married Julia Bard
Ruby Celestial (1855-1881), whose married name
    was Card

* The grandparents, aunts and uncles described by Laura Ingalls Wilder in the "Little House" books.

42

The Quiner-Holbrook family, late 1850s. Left to right: Frederick Holbrook, Tom Quiner, Lottie Holbrook, Charlotte Quiner Holbrook. Original at Laura Ingalls Wilder Home, Mansfield.

Henry Newton Quiner (1809-1844) and Charlotte Wallis Tucker (1809-1884) were married in New Haven, Connecticut in 1831. (Grandparents of Laura Ingalls Wilder).

Their children were:
Martha Morse (1832-1836)
Joseph C. (1834-1862), who married Nancy Frank (Joseph died from wounds at Shiloh)
Henry Odin (1835-1886), who married Polly Ingalls
Martha Jane (1837-1927), who married Charles C. Carpenter
Caroline Lake (1839-1924), who married Charles P. Ingalls
Eliza Ann (1842-1931), who married Peter R. Ingalls
Thomas Lewis (1844-1903), who married Lillian Hill

* * *

Charlotte Tucker Quiner's second marriage to Frederick Holbrook occurred on June 2, 1849. Their child was:
Charlotte E. (1854 - ?), who married Henry Moore.

APPENDIX
Letters From The Little Houses

Two traits of the Ingalls family make them a biographer's dream: they wrote letters extensively to one another, and they kept much of their correspondence. There is no better way to piece together the later lives of the Little House characters than through their letters.

Pioneer life often necessitated a stoic attitude toward loss, separation and the inability to have close proximity to relatives. Since the Ingalls family history is one of frequent moves, leaving relatives behind sometimes meant that they would never meet again. To remedy this, the Ingallses and Quiners maintained a "circular" exchange between the various families for decades. Each branch wrote its news, sent the letter on to the next family, and when the rounds were made, the process started again. Laura Ingalls Wilder's family were participants.

Little House book readers have wondered why there was not more visiting between Laura Ingalls Wilder and her family after she left South Dakota to move to Mansfield in 1894. Whatever the reason (probably finances and difficulty of travel were issues) letters exchanged between Laura and her family indicate their strong bond, their concern for each other, and their hunger for news.

After the three Ingalls sisters left home, Ma's trips to the post office often brought mail from the girls. She read every letter aloud to Mary. The "penny post card" was very popular in the early 1900s. Quick updates were penned on the reverse of decorative cards, or on actual photos in post card format. Ma and her daughters often exchanged these post cards. A visitor to the Ingalls home recalled that the drop leaf desk in the dining room was laden with piles of these post cards.

What happened to most of the family correspondence which ended up at the Third Street house? No one really knows. That there was a glut of saved mail was certain …. letters from Mary's college days, letters from Laura en route to Missouri, letters from Grace when she was away in college …. all these and more must have filled boxes and drawers. Some examples exist; most were destroyed when the home was cleared out in 1946. An eyewitness, who realized that the Ingalls family represented De Smet history, recalled blizzards of paper flying from the second floor windows into a truck bed bound for the town dump. A friend of Carrie's visited Aubrey Sherwood's newspaper office, realizing what had been lost. "Oh Aubrey, we should have saved those things," she mourned.

Through remaining examples of their letters, we hear the distant voices of the pioneering Ingalls family. Always evident in their writing is a deep affection which stretched between miles and years of separation. Here is a sampling of the Ingalls family's mail.

In 1908 Grace and Nate Dow visited the Pacific coast.

April 1, 1908

Dear Laura, Arrived in Portland this morning. Had a lovely trip. Hope to get a letter from you soon if you haven't forgotten me. Address Gervais Ore. Care of A. Bump. Grace

*****

April 13, 1908

Dear Carrie, Here in Salem having a day of it. Why don't you write? Having the time of my life. Will write soon. We can see Mt. Hood from our house in Gervais. Grace

*****

Carrie traveled extensively through the west during her career. While on her claim in western South Dakota she stayed connected with family through photo post cards, taken with her own camera.

Elbon, S.D.
May 2, 1908

Dear Mother, Here I am at home. Wish you could see the inside. I am going to take one of "the interior" soon. Everybody well. Had a great storm but the weather is growing warmer now. Am going to commence to "sod up" the house today. Got a letter from Grace. Will write soon.   Carrie

*****

De Smet
Dec. 12, '08

Dear Grace, I came through Manchester this morning only saw Mr. Rolfson to wave at. Could not send you word for it stormed and I will come up some morning before long. Everything fine. Carrie

*****

Manchester
March 15, '09

Addressed to De Smet

Dear Carrie, Our man skipped out. It is just as well. Costs us $1.50, but he wouldn't work for less than $30 for 3 months and 35 for 4 mo. Counting board and wash, he wanted $50. Crazy Ike. I'm getting 20 eggs a day now.   Grace

45

Addressed to Pedro, S.D. (September, 1909)

Dear Carrie, In De Smet today. Your hat will be sent by express Monday. Hope you will like it. Same old feather. Folks are well.... We came down with Raphel & twelve head of cattle (fat) today. Have sent for some furs. Am going to have a new coat when I get the samples. Ma is making catsup. Grace

*****

Sept. 9, 1909

Dear Carrie, We are well. Were in De Smet Friday. Folks were well. Yesterday (Sunday) was auto day with us. Harry Frost's were here and Judge Green and wife and baby. Are you coming home this fall? We expect to thresh next week. The men are haying. Grace

*****

Pedro, S.D.
October 27, 1909

Dear Laura—Thought you would be glad to know I got the order for my patent to my farm Saturday. This is a real photograph of a claim shanty. How does it look? Carrie

De Smet So. Dak.
Jan 21-1910

Dear Laura - We are well but nearly buried in snow. We rec. your Christmas letter& gifts. Thank you very much. Also rec. card. Will write a letter soon. Carrie & Grace are well. Loving mother

*****

September 26, 1910

Dear Carrie, Nate has already sold some of the hay. We will have a man for a month yet to plow. We are getting lots of ripe tomatoes now. You bet they are good with sugar and cream. Have some. It seems like fall now. We had a light frost. Grace

May 3, 1911

Dear Carrie, We were disappointed not to get a letter from you this week. We are cleaning house. Gave a white coat to the kitchen ceiling and a brown and tan paper on the walls—a great improve-

ment. Will be all thru this week. Grace & Nate were down a week ago...Grace has the prettiest hat in town. Got it of Miss Jessen ....
All well. Lovingly, Mother

*****

(1911, addressed to Carrie in De Smet)

Nate got a tea kettle down to Robinson's...and forgot to get it this time. Would you just as soon get it and take it up to the house?
I'm afraid they'll forget it if we wait too long. It's a big green enamel one...I got my cream but not any announcement yet. Grace

*****

June 22, 1911

(Addressed to Carrie in De Smet from Manchester)

Don't believe we will be able to get down right away. It's too hot to put the big horses on the road. Can't you come down on the train—freight—or someway soon? Nate has to plow his corn again soon. I was surprised when I heard you had gone through last night. Doesn't everything look lovely and prosperous? Grace

*****

This letter was written a month after Carrie's surprise wedding

Manchester, S.D.
September 17, 1912

Dear Carrie,
Your letter received. You see I got the paper. Much obliged. It is raining today so I have time to write. When it is nice weather I help Nate outdoors with the hay. We can't get a man just now.
Are going to thresh next week and I guess it will make me go some to get ready for them too...

You can answer on a separate slip of paper when you send the circulating letter. Be sure to write a good long letter. It will save writing two or three letters. I'll bet you are busy and glad you like the children. When you want to go away on a trip send them up to us. I'd like to have them for awhile.

Nate is feeling quite well but I will glad of those pine needles to try when he has a spell. I believe Harold will outgrow his asthma.
They most always do when they are little and it comes on them again. Nate had it when he was a little shaver and got over it until the last few years.

Nate listed the place last time we were in De Smet. Ma hated it terribly. Don't believe we will sell this fall tho. We could get settled somewhere and come back after the folks or perhaps you could bring them. We haven't sold yet and won't cross any bridges.

We went to the Fair last Wed. Enjoyed seeing the airships but everything was the same old thing.

47

I sent for my reading this morning when we were uptown. I ordered two magazines sent to ma.

Sam Howard was back for a couple of days. He was here Friday. Don't think he is making anymore than a living in the city.

I had a long letter from Mrs. Fuller. They are about to leave their claims. She is going to Saskatoon to Tom's folks. Will stop in Minneapolis and get some clothes. Says she hasn't anything. Going to have a black satin dress and a black and white one piece dress & long black coat to travel. She says she hopes you have the best man in the world. You deserve the best.

I suppose you have a plain ring now to hold up that beauty of a ring...Does Dave have a horse & buggy so you can drive?

Don't hold up the circulating letter too long. Is this the missing slip you wanted me to send? You didn't say anything about my pretty post card.

Lots of love,
Grace

*****

Caroline Ingalls sent birthday greetings to her sister Martha Carpenter, who lived in Plainview, Minnesota

Nov 4—1912

Dear Sister — You are soon to pass another milestone on life's journey. The 75th one. Look! I am following close behind you! Does it seem possible that we are so old? May you see many returns of the day is the wish of your loving sister Caroline. Circular is here.

*****

De Smet,
February 2, 1914

(To Laura)

Dear Daughter, I will write only a few lines as I see Mary has written quite a long letter. I send you for a birthday gift a little piece for your table. I imagine the mat will be suitable for your meat platter in these days of high price of meat. Loving mother

*****

Rocky Ridge Farm,
12/27/20

(Letter fragment from Laura)

Dear Mother and Sisters:

We were glad to get your letter Grace. It came on Christmas Day. Manly and I spent the day by ourselves, with roast chicken and dressing, mashed Irish potatoe, baked sweet potatoe, brown bread, white bread, blackberry jelly, doughnuts, sweet potatoe pie (in place of pumpkin pie), cheese and coffee for dinner. After dinner we sat by the fire in the fireplace and read and looked at our Christmas cards and letters. Then later we popped corn over the fire and ate apples and walnuts and corn. We did not give each other presents of any value. I had made Manly a scrap book of clippings he was particularly fond of....

*****

In November, 1932 Carrie referred to the presidential election which Franklin D. Roosevelt won. Carrie and the Wilders voted for FDR.

Dear Laura and Manley, To let you know everyone is OK...Am with you on the election, but what is going to happen after it is all over? Just about winter up here. Aubrey Sherwood mentioned Rose's Saturday Eve Post. Just called attention to it, will send clipping. Will write tomorrow. Love, Carrie

*****

September 22, 1933

Dear Carrie, Manly is sending the pears today by express to Hill City. Hope they reach you all right. They must stand awhile before they are good to eat, but cook all right now.
Will ans. your letter soon. Love, Laura

*****

Sept. 28 (1933)

Dear Manley & Laura: The pears came this afternoon, not even a dent in them, and such a lot. No rain right here yet. It will be snow now if it comes. This is the place in the road Manley where the car wanted to run backward remember? The fence was put in after this was taken Laura. Will write soon. Love, Carrie.

*****

A note from Carrie to Laura in spring, 1939.

Laura do you suppose Rose has any clothes she is giving to charity? If she has do you think she would send them to me? It would save me buying some things. Now if you rather not— don't say anything about it—and above all don't send me any of yours. I can get along. I just thought if she was doing that I certainly would like to be the charity.

During the writing of her books, Carrie supplied a family songbook for Laura's reference. The Laura Ingalls mentioned in the next letter was a renowned aviatrix.

49

Keystone, S.D.
August 6, 1940

Dear Laura:

Was glad to get your letter. Your questions do not bother me, only in the way that I wonder why I cannot answer them.

I believe we sang the same pieces (hymns) in Sunday school that were used in church, it has been in later years where they got to thinking the old hymns were too slow and solemn for the younger generation...I remember all those and a few more [Carrie refers to the hymn book she is sending to Laura]...some of those I do not know certainly have queer expression...Of course they were written before 1871, they must have been picked for the best and more modern, though of course they did not say "modern" then.

If you do not get what you want from Vinton, Iowa, you could fall back on the old records of Dakota Territory, could you not? Your book will be all right, I know.

They had an Air meet ...at Spearfish two weeks ago, a "Holliwood groupe" that gave exhibitions, that greatest known man stunt flyer, and that jumper, etc. were there and so was Laura Ingalls, she and the stunt flyer gave "dog fight" in the air. I telephoned her at the airport there. She said she had no idea I was so near, but that the "Holliwood groupe" had to stay together they were on schedule time (and pay, I suppose) and she had "only a plane" and there was no landing field at Keystone so she could not take the time to come. They say she was great. So she must be in the movies, for the Holliwood bunch had a manager, the paper said. Spearfish is about a two hour run from here. I did not have the money....to go up...She might not have wanted me to to...though of course she said so.

It's awful dry here, all the wells are going dry, mine went dry last week. I get drinking water across at that tourist camp, they still have it. If it rains this fall the water will come back I think.

Have not had time to think up about politics but will write you later, if I think I know anything about them... Love, Carrie

*****

One of Laura's last letters to Carrie

Mansfield, MO
May 21, 1945

Dear Carrie,

This is just a note to tell you I have sent De Smet Cemetery Association $5.00 in your name and mine for care of Ingalls family lot. So you need not bother to think about it.

We are having an awful spring. First planting of potatoes and garden seed rotted in the ground it was so cold and wet. Since then the ground has not been dry enough to plow. Corn can't be planted; hay spoils before it drys and it looks as though we will be needing more food than will be raised this year.

Well! The big oak trees in front and west of the house are all cleared away. A cyclone did it. It uprooted them, just tore them up by the roots. It tore out a big walnut tree by the barn and split the elm by the iris bed. The great, old oak close in front of the house was broken in pieces and trunk split the whole length. Some shingles were torn off the house and the big south window in the front room was blown out, but we were lucky the house didn't go. A good many houses did, and people were hurt. It was two weeks before we could get the big trees out of our driveway so we could get out. Telephone and electric wires were down two weeks. Am still looking for that letter you were writing at once.

Lots of Love, Laura

(The tornado passed through the day Roosevelt died.)

*****

A postcard showing the Ingalls home on Third Street in De Smet.

ABOUT THE AUTHOR

William Anderson has spent many years researching and writing about the people and places of the "Little House" books. He has been active in the preservation of the Ingalls-Wilder sites in De Smet and Mansfield. In addition to writing the *"Laura Ingalls Wilder Family Series"*, he is author of *A Little House Sampler, Laura Ingalls Wilder Country, Laura Ingalls Wilder A Biography,* and *A Little House Reader* (all published by Harper Collins).

He has also written about a variety of topics in such magazines as *The Saturday Evening Post, American History Illustrated, The Horn Book, The Christian Science Monitor* and others.

Some of his other books include: *The World of the Trapp Family, River Boy:The Story of Mark Twain,* and *M is for Mount Rushmore.*

Visit him on the web at:
www.williamandersonbooks.com